Brave Lady

*To Linda & Leo
Fellow Dog park
friends,
Stacy & Lady
27 Oct '16*

Brave Lady By Stacy Brooks

Copyright © 2012
All rights reserved. No part of this publication may be reproduced or transmitted in any form or by any means, electronic or mechanical including photography, without permission in working from Stacy Brooks, Cradleboard Interpretive Services. 1st edition 2013

She grew up alone and afraid.
Can she learn not to be so scared?
It's not easy to do.

Lady was living in an empty lot, like a ghost.
She was a shadow under the sagebrush.

or a flash from around the corner.

Lady ran whenever a person came near.
No one could touch her.

Lady was hungry sometimes.
She was more brave if she might get food.
Food attracted her to people…just not too close.

Terra saw her hiding and scared.
No one should have to live like a ghost.
Terra wanted to help.

Terra made her come closer to get food,

little

by little

by little.

Lady started following Terra to

the store

the post office

and just for fun.

Slowly, Lady had to come inside to eat.
When Terra closed the door, Lady wanted to run.

but she came back.

Terra made her stay inside

longer

and longer

and longer.

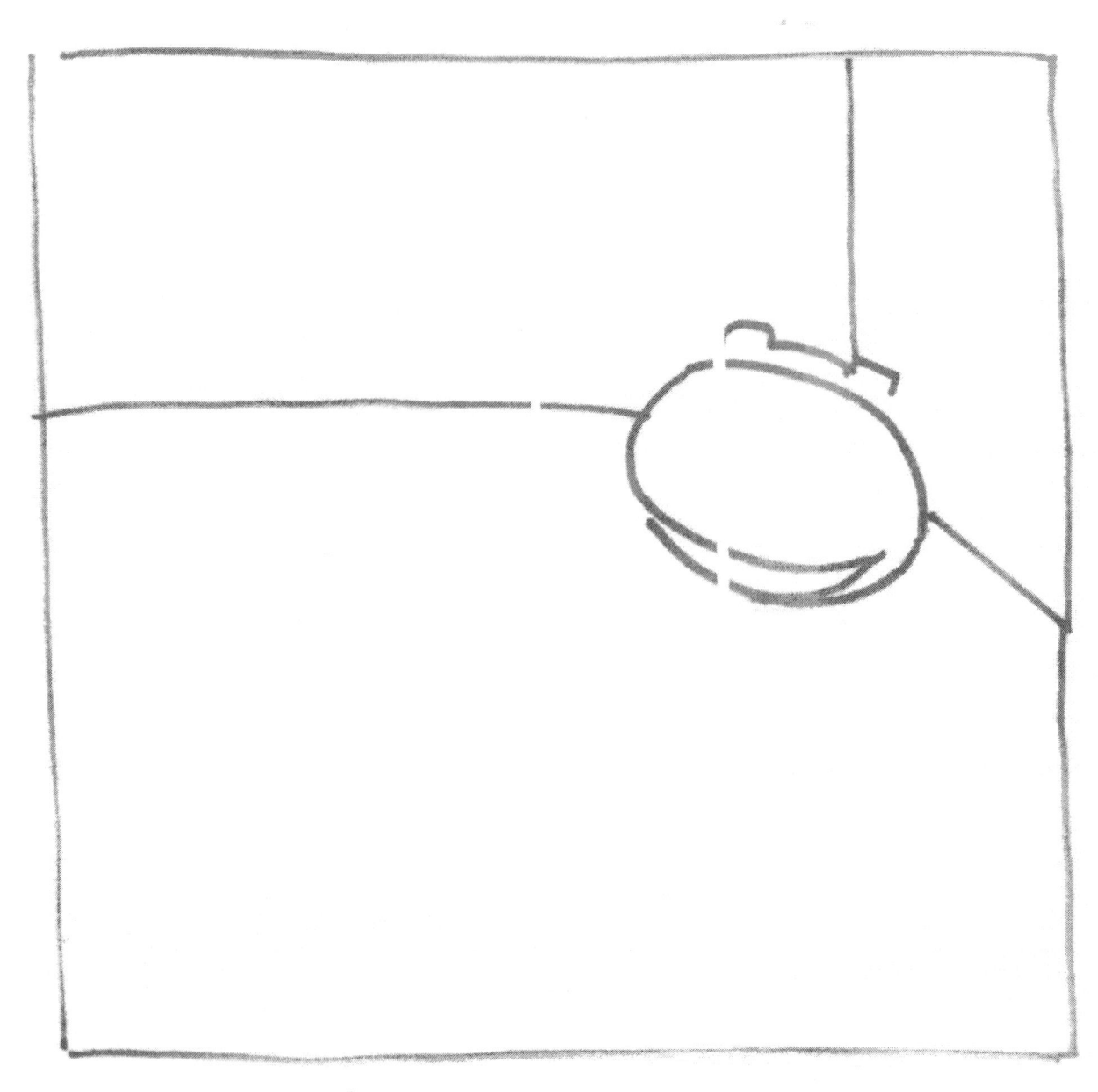

At first, Lady tried to hide.

One day, Terra sat close
and touched Lady very gently

little

by little

by little

Lady wasn't so afraid.

Lady found a friend

and a home.

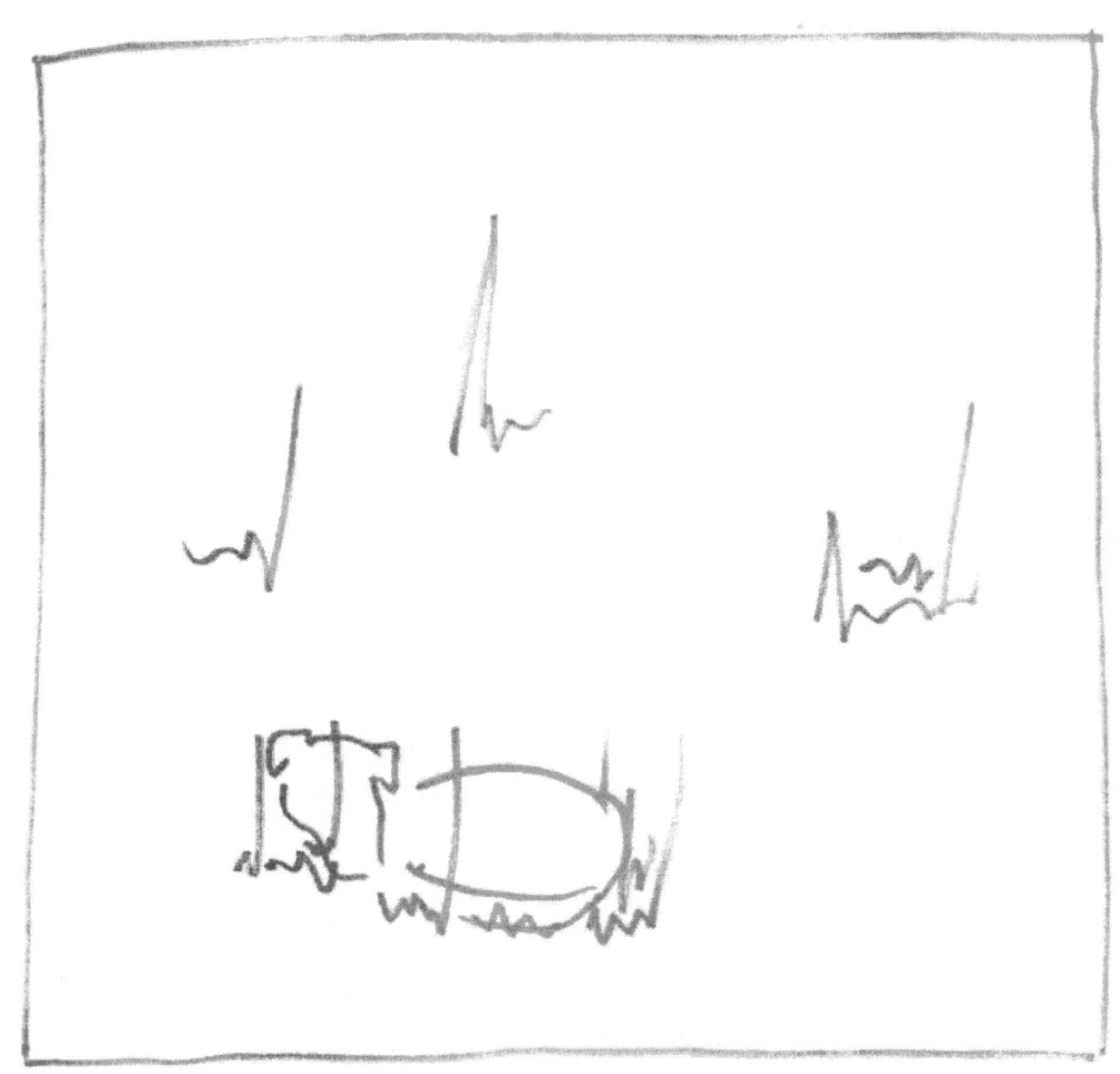

Have you ever been scared
and found out you didn't need to be?
Lady learned how to trust...slowly.

Brave Lady

Made in the USA
Middletown, DE
15 October 2016